Directions for Using the Contents of the Portable Horse Medicine Chest

Directions for Using the Contents of the Portable Horse Medicine Chest:

Adapted for India

W. MOORCROFT

GYAN

Published by

Gyan Publishing House
5, Ansari Road
Daryaganj, New Delhi-110002
Phone: 011-47034999, 9811692060
E-mail: books@gyanbooks.com

Distribution Network
gyanbooks.com
India, USA, Canada, UK, Australia

ISBN: 978-93-7133-704-5 (PB)

First Published, 1795

2nd Impression 2025

Printed at: Gyan Press, Delhi.

DIRECTIONS FOR USING THE CONTENTS OF THE PORTABLE HORSE MEDICINE CHEST: ADAPTED FOR INDIA

Author: W. MOORCROFT

DIRECTIONS

FOR

USING THE CONTENTS

OF THE

PORTABLE

HORSE MEDICINE CHEST,

ADAPTED FOR INDIA;

AND

PREPARED BY

W. MOORCROFT,

VETERINARY SURGEON,

OXFORD-STREET, LONDON.

1795.

DIRECTIONS, &c.

OF THE FEET OF HORSES IN INDIA; OF THEIR MOST COMMON DEFECTS, AND OF THE MODES OF REMEDYING THEM.

THE Feet of Horses in general, in hot climates, are smaller than of those in colder regions. This arises partly from the breeds indigenous to hot countries being lighter and more active, and partly from the dryness and heat of the soil. Feet, which are either small or large in the extreme, are equally liable to diseases, although of different natures; and this in a much greater degree than those of a moderate size.

The diseases to which a small Foot gives a disposition, and which are most common in India, are Contracted Heels,

Running Thrushes, Goat Hoofs, and Fleshy Frogs.

As this Essay is intended to apply only to the Horses in India, it would be out of place to enter into a detail of the diseases peculiar to those of temperate or cold countries. Nor would it be less inconsistent with the plan I have laid down, to enter into a minute detail of the causes of the diseases incident to the climate in question; I have therefore contented myself with supposing the diseases to be known to exist, and with pointing out the most obvious modes of removing them, without entering into a description of their symptoms.

Here, perhaps, it may not be improper to say a few words relative to the general treatment of a sound Foot, and of the means of retaining it in a healthy state.

OF PREPARING A SOUND FOOT FOR A SHOE.

The parts which are concerned in this preparation are those which constitute the bottom of the Foot; viz. the Crust, Bars, Sole, and Frog. The Crust, or outer edge of the bottom of the Foot, is intended to repose upon the ground, and from its structure is liable to be rubbed or worn away. To supply the loss produced by violent friction, its growth is quick, proceeding from above downwards. This part, by being covered with a semicircular bar of iron, is prevented from coming in contact with the ground, and consequently from being worn. Hence the Crust, in a Horse which has been shod for some time, is found to exceed the level of the Sole. When it has passed above half an inch beyond the level of the last-mentioned part, and in many instances before it has proceeded so far, it loses somewhat of its solidity, and becomes by degrees more or less crumbly and brittle.

It has then not only the inconvenience of not presenting a basis sufficiently stable for fixing a Shoe upon, but likewise by its weight, and by lengthening the extremity, it renders the Horse more liable to trip and stumble. In fact, it becomes necessary to lower it, and this is to be done by paring it within an eighth of an inch to a level with the Sole.

The Sole is likewise intended to press against the ground, but not to so great an extent as the Crust, as is evident from its being hollow. The superfluous growth of this part was intended to have been removed, partly by friction, and partly by the lower surface losing its consistence, and detaching itself in the form of scales of a crumbly or mealy nature.

This process is frequently impeded, and in many instances completely prevented by the Shoe. The accumulation of this portion of Sole, which has lost its living principle, is injurious from its adding weight to the extremity. It has been imagined that it tended to the defence of the parts within the Hoof; but the living horny Sole is sufficient to answer this purpose. Were this not the case, the detaching process would not have been adopted. The Sole should, therefore, be cleared of all the scales or mealy substance; but as soon as the buttress reaches that surface which cuts toughly, it should be laid aside.

The Bars or Binders experience little wearing, and may without risk be cut horizontally to the level of the Sole; but are by no means to be scooped or hollowed out; as this lays a foundation for Contracted Heels, and other diseases.

The Frog in some Horses, when it has attained a certain size, by degrees separates in one layer from the new one, which is about to supply its place, and may be removed without difficulty. In others, it detaches itself by fragments, which require to be cut off. Generally speaking, it is a much better practice to confine the use of the Drawing Knife simply to removing whatever parts may be detached or rotten, and to render the surface even, than to imitate that of thinning the Frog, to give it a regular or agreeable shape at each time of shoeing.

To express what I have before stated more concisely, I recommend that

The Crust should be pared perfectly flat in its whole extent, nearly to a level with the Sole.

That the Sole be freed from the scaly substance, but that none of the tough and solid part be removed.

That the Bars be made level with the Sole, but not hollowed.

That the Frog be divested of its ragged surface, but not pared away.

I have thought it proper to send the

Shoe that appears most adapted to general use in India; which precludes the necessity of describing it.

OF CONTRACTED HEELS.

This defect is too well known to require a description. Although in many instances it may appear to be hereditary, yet it more frequently arises from an abuse of the buttress, and from narrow shoeing.

The Hoof may be considered as consisting of two elastic parts, viz. the Crust and the Sole, which have powers in opposition to each other; the Crust, from its form and structure, has a constant tendency to press inwards upon the parts which it covers, and therefore may be said to possess a power of contraction. The Sole appears as a wedge to keep the edges of the Crust at a distance from each other, and may thence be looked upon as having a power of dilatation.

The Bars and Frog should in this point of view be accounted as composing part of the Sole, and assisting in the same function, independent of that which is peculiar to each of them. Whilst these powers equally balance each other, contraction of the Heels (which are the parts of the Crust first disposed to shrink in) cannot possibly take place, nor can the Foot become flatter or wider. But if by accident or improper treatment either of these powers be weakened, the other remaining in full force, produces an alteration in the form of the Foot, in proportion to the part weakened. It happens, however, most frequently that the power of dilatation is that which suffers, from the Sole being too much pared, the Bars scooped out, the Frog cut away, and the Heels separated from it by an artificial and deep niche. This practice obtains too generally in England, and has made its way into India; for which reason I have dwelt longer upon it than the limits of this paper would otherwise have warranted.

Narrow Shoeing has been adduced as another cause of Contracted Heels; this, however, does not operate so frequently as that to which I have before alluded.

Much rest in the stable has likewise a tendency to produce the same effect.

OF THE MODE OF REMEDYING CONTRACTED HEELS.

Pare the Heels as low as they will bear, so that the Frog may come freely to the ground; shoe with Tips, or Half-moon Shoes, covering the Toes only; give much gentle exercise in soft ground, and keep the Foot as much as possible in a state of Moisture, by steeping it for an hour a day in lukewarm water.

In addition to these means, reducing the thickness of the Crust at the Heels will be found of use, as it will cause them to afford less resistance to the action of the Frog, which expands when it is pressed against the ground by the weight of the body, and which communicates part of its action to the Heels.

This expedient must, however, be used with great caution, as I have seen much deformity in the Foot produced by the Heel having been weakened too much, and too suddenly. After each steeping, the Crust may be scraped downwards with the edge of a piece of broken glass, or be slightly rasped; but if it give way in the slightest degree to strong pressure from the thumb, or if the Animal at such time should shew any sign of pain or uneasiness, it is a proof that too much has already been done.

Permanent Lameness is a very common effect of Contracted Heels, as are also Sandcracks and Corns.

The Remedies pointed out ought to be carried into execution as soon as a disposition to contract is perceived, as the recovery of Heels which have been long and to a considerable degree contracted, is a work of much time and perseverance.

OF RUNNING THRUSHES.

Contracted Heels and Running Thrushes are frequently found to exist together. When the Frog is prevented from coming into contact with the ground, either by the Heels having been suffered to become too high, or from the long continued use of Caulkers or thick-heeled Shoes, it usually becomes spongy and rotten. Long standing in wet Litter likewise conduces to the same end.

Whilst there does not exist much Rottenness or Discharge, it does not appear to produce any material inconvenience to the Animal; but when these are both considerable, and of long standing, Lameness comes on occasionally, from the parts underneath being bruised against hard ground or stones. Contracted Heels are rendered more difficult of Cure by it, and not unfrequently it leads to Canker and permanent Lameness.

An idea has obtained, that like some disagreeable diseases to which mankind are incident, it relieved the Constitution from other complaints under which it might have laboured, and that the sudden drying up of Thrushes was productive of both general and local indisposition; as of Fever, Inflammation of the Lungs, and most particularly of the Eyes. The first part of this idea is a mistake, and with regard to the latter, although some mischief may occasionally have happened from the sudden suppression of a Discharge to which the parts have been long accustomed, yet under proper precautions, the Cure of Thrushes of long existence and malignity ought always to be attempted, and may be effected without danger.

OF THE CURE OF RUNNING THRUSHES.

Pare off the ragged rotten Surface of the Frog; clean every part of it thoroughly with dry Tow; then dip a little Tow in the Thrush Mixture, after it has been well shaken up, and press it rather tight into the Clefts from which the Discharge proceeds. This should be done every evening, and be continued for a month, after all Discharge has stopped. Should the Thrush be of long standing, or the Discharge considerable, give half a Diuretic Ball (No. V.) once every four or six days during this treatment, and even for three weeks after the Discharge has entirely ceased, and the Frog become firm and dry.

In the course of this treatment the Horse should be allowed to stand as little as possible in wet places, as nothing retards the Cure more than Moisture.

Lowering the Heels, so that the Frog

may bear upon the ground, and Shoeing with Tips, or short Shoes, are eminently advantageous in promoting the Recovery.

Should Swellings of the Legs, or Inflammation of the Eyes, or of any other Part of the Body, come on without any obvious cause, within a month from the Cure of the Thrush, take away from Two to Four Quarts of Blood, according to the Strength or Condition of the Horse, and give a whole Diuretic Ball every fourth night, till the complaint goes off.

OF GOAT HOOFS.

By this term is meant such Feet as have the fore Part of the Hoof falling almost perpendicularly from the Coronet to the Toe, instead of stretching obliquely forwards, and the Heels round, straight, and deep, standing as high as the Toe. The circumference of the upper and lower edges of the Hoof is nearly of equal dimensions.

The Sole is much more hollow than in any other Hoof. Feet of this description have a disposition to Thrushes and Canker. They likewise bring on weakness of the Fetlock Joints, and sometimes obstinate and even incurable Lameness, by compressing the parts within the Hoof. This form of Hoof is in some instances hereditary, but generally is acquired. Either case is susceptible, if not of absolute remedy, at least of material alleviation.

The same mode of treatment as that for Contracted Heels is applicable here; except that the Heels must be lowered by degrees, as the sudden removal of much Heel at one time, would dispose to injuries of the back Tendons of the Leg. The Toe should be preserved, and the Shoe should sit rather full, or in other words, pass a little beyond this part.

OF FLESHY FROGS.

When, with an over proportion of Frog, this part is found to yield readily to slight pressure, it is said to be Fleshy.

Fleshy Frogs usually accompany such Feet as are disposed to be flat, and where the Soles are thin, and the Heels low and weak. Generally speaking, this is a natural defect, which by proper care is not followed by any ill effects, but which by mismanagement frequently leads to disease.

As the Horny Covering in this species of Frog is much more soft and thin than in a well constituted Hoof, the parts contained within it are less completely guarded, and consequently more liable to be injured than when the Frog possesses the usual consistence.

Thus they are subject to Wounds and Bruises, which are followed by malignant

Thrushes, having a disposition to become cankerous.

OF THE TREATMENT OF FLESHY FROGS.

In Running Thrushes it must be observed, that I have laid much stress upon the circumstance of bringing the Frog in contact with the ground, and thus causing it to support a large share of the weight of the Body. By constant pressure it gradually acquires solidity. This mode might, therefore, be thought applicable to the constitution of Frog now under consideration, but it has been found that it will not bear such a degree of pressure as the former without inconvenience; therefore the Heels of the Shoes should be so raised, that the Frog may be only just upon a level with them, and a pledget of tow dipped in the Thrush Mixture should be applied to it every evening.

The Heels should be suffered to grow

to nearly the same height with the Frog; and the Toe should be kept short.

OF HORSES WHICH CUT.

This defect may arise from want of sufficient action in the upper part of the limb, from turning out the Toes, or from bad Shoeing.

From which of these causes it may derive, it may be lessened, or be entirely removed by judicious treatment.

In general, the inner quarter of the Feet of Horses which cut, either before or behind, should be suffered to grow high, whilst the outer one should be reduced to a level with the Sole.

The inner branch of the Shoe should be somewhat narrow, thick at the Heel, and be gradually diminished towards the Toe; whilst the outer branch should be only of an ordinary thickness.

The inner branch should be fullered, or

grooved fine, near the outer edge, and be what is called feathered; that is to say, the bottom of the branch should not be flat, but from the fuller should be sloped off inwards, so that it may form a narrow ridge, corresponding with that on the inner and lower edge of the Shoe, and which should become broader as it approaches the Toe.

The outer edge of this branch, in general, should follow the line of the Crust, but in those Horses which cut much, it should keep within, rather than pass beyond it; taking care, however, that it rest not altogether upon the Sole.

By this means, whilst the Animal is standing still, the Toe will be turned a little inwards, and this determination will influence it during its passage through the air, in the different paces.

ON HORSES WHICH OVER-REACH.

Horses which have long Pasterns are most particularly subject to this imperfection.

It appears to be owing to the Fore Feet remaining too long upon the ground, whilst the Hind Feet are removed from it too quickly.

To obviate this, the Heels of the Fore Feet should be lowered as much as they will bear, and Shoes with thin Heels should be made use of. By this means the Flexor Muscles, or those which bend the Leg, will suffer more extension, and to relieve themselves will contract sooner, and thus cause the Foot to dwell a shorter time upon the ground than would happen were the Heels suffered to remain high.

It is obvious that an opposite plan should be adopted with regard to the

Hind Feet; and if the Heels do not grow sufficiently high, the Heels of the Shoes must be proportionally thickened. This will cause the Hind Legs to dwell a longer time upon the ground, and thus their interference with the Fore ones will be prevented.

OF THE DISEASES AND ACCIDENTS MOST FREQUENT TO HORSES IN INDIA.

OF WOUNDS NEAR THE FOOT, BY TREADS AND OVER-REACHES.

These injuries usually admit of an easy Cure, if early attention be paid to them.

When a Horse has received a Wound near the Foot, and there is reason to suspect that sand or other matter may have gone in, let the part be well washed with warm water; then bring the edges together; apply a piece of Tow dipped in the Tincture for Wounds, and bind it on. The first dressing should be suffered to remain undisturbed as long as it will stick; then, if the skin should not be healed, cover the part with Tow, moistened with the Drying Mixture. Repeat this every second day, till the skin becomes hard.

OF SWELLINGS IN THE BACK PART OF THE LEGS, COMMONLY CALLED CLAPS IN THE BACK SINEWS.

Horses which have long and yielding Pasterns, with low Heels, and long Toes, are most exposed to accidents of this nature, which, if not timely remedied, frequently prove very difficult of cure.

As soon as the Swelling is perceived, shave or clip the hair close to the Leg, and apply as many Leeches to the swollen part as will cover it: when they drop off, place the Leg in a pail of lukewarm water, and keep it nearly of the same temperature.

This should be continued for about an hour.

Mix two tea-spoonfulls of the Powder for Strains (No. II.) with a tea-cupfull of Vinegar, and a quart of soft Water; stir into it as much Barley or Maize Flour as may be sufficient to make a Poultice of a proper consistence. Spread this about an inch thick on old linen, and apply largely round the Leg, observing that the Bandage be not tighter than may be absolutely necessary for keeping it on. Repeat the Poultice twice a day, and continue it till the Heat and Tenderness subside. When the Inflammation shall have disappeared, and there only remains a Fulness in the Part, a Bandage of fine Flannel, well wetted with the Mixture before mentioned, should be bound round the part, and kept constantly moist.

In common cases, this treatment will generally prove adequate to a Cure, with the addition of Rest.

If there be much Pain and Lameness, it would be adviseable to take away from One to Three Quarts of Blood from the Neck Vein, and to administer a Purging Ball (No. IV.) which should be repeated in eight or ten days, if the Soreness and Swelling do not go off.

Much Rest is essentially necessary.

If the Inflammation should not run high, a Diuretic Ball (No. V.) every third evening, until the part is less sensible under pressure and diminishes in point of size, will be found sufficient.

In many instances, these accidents leave a Fulness and Weakness in the Leg, to which Blistering may occasionally be used with advantage; but which in others only gives way to judicious Firing.

OF THE BURSAUTEE.

This Disease is so called from making its appearance in the rainy season.

As far as I am able to judge of it, from the accounts I have received, it has not any strict affinity with any Disorder to which Horses in Europe are incident. In some respects, it seems to resemble the Farcy, in others the Grease ; but on the whole appears more allied to the former than to the latter.

From never having had an opportunity of being an eye-witness of this Complaint, I cannot presume to prescribe a specific treatment for it ; but should recommend the following to be put in practice.

In the very early stages, when the Disease begins to shew itself by Ulcers in the Skin, near the Foot, or in any other part of the Body, it would be well to destroy them, by the application of a Hot Iron, care being taken that the Burning do not extend too far. In other words, the surface of the Ulcer, however extensive it may be, should be completely burnt; but the adjacent sound parts should be as little injured as possible.

After this operation, the parts affected should be wrapped up in the Poultice, as for Strains, where it can conveniently be applied, as in the extremities. Where the Ulcers are situate upon such surfaces as do not admit of the application of a Poultice, the Ointment (No. I.) may be found a convenient substitute.

If Fever should accompany the first attack, to any great extent, it might not be improper to take away from Two to Five Quarts of Blood, and to give a Purge (No. IV.) and repeat it every six or seven days, until the Fever subside.

When much Fever does not exist, the Purge alone may be sufficient.

As soon as the dead surfaces of the Ulcers are cast off, the Sores may be touched once a day, for three or four days, with the Drying Mixture; and when they reach the level of the Skin, they may be covered with the Drying Powder, as directed under that article.

Much exercise in the open air, when practicable, might prove conducive to recovery; and even it might in some instances not be improper to carry it so far as to produce Sweating; but of this I speak with diffidence.

I cannot with propriety hazard any conjecture respecting the cause of this complaint, from want of sufficient acquaintance with all the circumstances connected with it.

OF THE COLIC OR GRIPES.

The Colic usually arises from mechanical or chemical causes, producing either Obstruction or Irritation in some part of the Intestinal Canal.

This complaint is divided ordinarily into two kinds, viz. the Dry and Common Gripes.

OF THE DRY GRIPES.

This is generally attended with violent Purging, cold Sweats, and Convulsions; and in Bengal frequently proves fatal.

It is particularly prevalent in the rainy season; and is commonly imputed to an Herb said to be poisonous, which springs at this time. However, as the stomachs of those Horses which have died in consequence of this disorder, uniformly appeared to have suffered much from the presence of Bots, and in many instances to have been absolutely perforated by them, it is more allowable to attribute the disorder to this cause than to any vegetable poison.

The limits of this paper will not admit of entering into a minute account of the natural history of this destructive animal, however interesting it might be. Let it suffice then to observe, that a kind of two-winged Fly, somewhat smaller than the common Bee, although much resembling it in appearance, during the summer months in Europe, deposites its Eggs upon the Hair of Horses, to which they firmly adhere.

Horses bite and lick their Skins, and take off these Eggs, which are swallowed. They hatch in the stomach; and by means of two hooks of horn with which they are provided, they attach themselves to its inner surface, where they remain, as it were at anchor, for nine or ten months. Having by this time acquired a size and strength fitting them for change, they disentangle their hooks from the stomach, and having lost their hold, are carried down the Intestines, and evacuated with the excrement.

During the spring months Bots are

frequently perceived sticking to the verge of the Anus, as if unwilling to quit their former habitation. After having fallen to the ground, they creep under a leaf or a stone, or secrete themselves in crevices; their skins harden and become brown; for some time they appear motionless, and at a period which I have not exactly ascertained, but which I believe a short one, a Fly emerges from each Bot, leaving a horny husk behind.

The Bot Worm, when full grown, is about an inch in length, of a conical form, about the size of the barrel of a goose-quill at its thickest part. Its colour is a yellowish red. Its skin is hard, and has nine or more rings, which are each beset with a double row of short horny points. Nature appears to have been unusually attentive to the preservation of this animal, and notwithstanding the variety of Medicines held out as destructive to it, I must confess that I am not experimentally acquainted with more than one which appears to have any specific power over it, after it has acquired a certain size.

And even this remedy has not yet stood a test sufficiently strong to admit of its being offered with confidence to the public. From what I have observed, it appears that Bots produce dangerous symptoms during the whole of their stay in the Stomach, only at two periods, viz. soon after they are hatched and begin to wound the Stomach, by fixing their hooks in its inner Surface; and again, when struggling to detach themselves from their hold, which on account of the form and peculiar mechanism of the hooks, must be a work of great exertion.

The Stomach, after a certain time, it is to be presumed, becomes accustomed to their continual irritation, and accommodates itself to it whilst it continues within certain bounds; but when it goes beyond these, as at the periods alluded to, a disorder is brought on which frequently proves destructive. In the interval between these periods, I do not recollect having seen any symptoms which I could attribute to the Bots; and there is much reason to believe that they remain fixed to the spot to which they first attached themselves, each occupying only a very small surface of the Stomach, as they may be said to stand on their heads. There is indeed not any necessity for their shifting of place, as they always find a sufficient nourishment in contact with their mouths. From this sketch it is obvious, that it is a matter of much importance to prevent the Eggs of the Bot Fly being introduced into the Stomach. With this view, I should recommend that observations be made respecting the time of the existence of the Animal in the Fly shape, which may be known by Eggs being found upon the Hair. These Eggs are very small, of a bright yellow colour, and of an oval form. As soon as they are discovered, it would be well to impregnate the Hair of the Horses with some substance that may prove offensive to the Fly.

In some parts of Germany, it has long been a practice among farmers to rub their Horses in the Summer with the leaves of strong-smelling vegetables, as elder, wormwood, laurel, but more especially with those of the walnut-tree, in order to prevent their being teazed by the attacks of the common Horse Fly.

Flies in general have an aversion to oil; but I should fear, that brushing the Hair with it, might prove injurious on another account.

When Eggs are perceived upon the Hair, they should be carefully taken off; and when no more are to be observed, a Purgative should be given, and repeated in eight or ten days. This would probably destroy, or dislodge the animals when only just hatched.

When a Horse is attacked with the Dry Gripes, a large quantity of Olive Oil, or other mild Vegetable Oil, should immediately be given, to the amount of three or four quarts; a Glyster, consisting of a handful of Salt, dissolved in two quarts of warm Water, should be given, and repeated every hour.

OF THE COMMON GRIPES.

The symptoms of this disorder are so well known, as to render any minute description of them superfluous.

The most common causes are much dry food, without a due proportion of water; by which means Obstruction takes place: or by the use of such food as throws out much air whilst in the Intestines.

As this complaint generally appears

when new Gram is made use of, in many cases it may be attributed to the Fermentation, which begins whilst it is soaking. I would therefore recommend it to be steeped double the usual time; or if this be inconvenient, that the water be changed as often as it becomes sour.

When the complaint arises in consequence of any mechanical Obstruction, it is usually preceded by Costiveness, and occasionally attended with a Suppression of Urine. The symptoms in this case are generally mild at first, and gradually increase, till either the Obstruction be removed, or terminates in death.

When the symptoms are very violent at first, and come on suddenly without any previous Costiveness, it is presumable that the complaint arises from some ligature being made upon the Intestines, or to their being painfully distended with air; in the latter case, in addition to the common symptoms, the Belly becomes full and hard soon after the first attack; whereas in the first instance, although the Belly does swell, yet it increases but slowly.

To which of these causes the complaint may be owing, the following treatment is equally applicable.

Bleed from two to six, or even eight quarts, if the symptoms be very violent, and the Horse strong. Then dissolve one of the Colic Balls in a pint of warm Water, and give by means of a horn. Wisp the Belly very well, and give a Glyster made of two quarts of warm Water, and half a pound of common Salt, every half hour till the Gripings go off. The Ball may be repeated every hour. Be particularly attentive to drench the Horse with large quantities of thin warm Gruel.

Gentle walking will be of service in shortening the Fit, but the Animal must by no means be rode violently.

When the disease resists these means,

Tobacco Smoke, introduced by a long flexible tube of leather, frequently proves advantageous. Blistering the Belly in obstinate cases may be had recourse to; and if the complaint do not yield, the Belly and Legs may be repeatedly dashed with cold Water.

OF THE WORM IN THE EYE.

This is a complaint unknown in Europe, but which has been seen in North America, and is common in Bengal.

The Worm is about an inch, or somewhat more in length, very thin, and moves about nimbly in the aqueous humour, or that which occupies the fore part of the Eye.

Its presence soon renders this organ opaque, and Blindness ensues.

It rarely happens to both Eyes at the same time.

An Opening should be made in the Eye, which at once may give vent to the aqueous humour, and afford an exit to the Worm.

This operation requires some steadiness and address in the execution. The Horse should be cast; and when the Head is properly secured, the Operator should, with the fingers of the left hand, supposing it to be the left Eye which is to be the subject of the operation, press upon the Eye from the Eye-pit, so as to steady it, which however is not easily effected. With his thumb he should raise the upper Eyelid, whilst an Assistant presses down the lower; then holding a lancet with its edges standing upwards and downwards, and consequently the flat part towards the Eye, he should push it into the clear part, at the outer corner, just before the white part, and carry it horizontally forwards; taking care not to give any other direction to the instrument. As soon as the lancet has penetrated a quarter of an inch into the Eye, let it be quickly withdrawn, and in the same direction in which it was introduced.

This operation, performed by a very ingenious gentleman, to whom I am indebted for many communications on the subject of Horses in India, has frequently been followed by the most complete success. The Eye, afterwards covered with a few doubles of linen, moistened with the Eye Water afterwards to be mentioned, will soon recover its original integrity.

OF SPAVINS, RINGBONES, AND SPLINTS.

The seat and nature of each of these complaints are presumed to be known.

Shave or clip the hair from the part, and rub with a little of the Blistering Ointment. Secure the Horse's Head for 24 hours, so that he may not gnaw the part blistered. On the second morning wash with warm water and soft soap, scrape off whatever scurf may remain, until the whole of the blistered surface be completely cleaned; then cover with the Wound Ointment. In four or five days the part will be sufficiently healed to admit of a second Blister, which must be managed as before directed. In bad cases it may be well to blister a third time, but then a longer interval must be allowed.

In recent diseases of this nature, blistering and rest will prove adequate to a Cure; but in those which are inveterate, it would be well to make use of Firing.

OF SWELLED TESTICLES.

When, in consequence of any injury done to them, the Testicles swell, inflame, hang lower than usual, and produce Fever, let two Quarts of Blood or more be taken away, bathe the parts frequently with the Mixture prescribed for Strains, &c.; give a Purgative, and keep the Horse quiet. If the Horse is so quiet as to bear a suspending Bandage, it would much contribute to a speedy recovery. Let a Crupper be put on, either fastened forwards by a Surcingle or a Breast-plate; make a Linen Bandage about a foot in breadth, resembling a Roman T; let the heads of the Bandage pass from underneath the Belly to the Loins, where it may be fastened to the Crupper. The tail part of the Bandage should be brought backwards between the Legs, where it may be split, and each piece may be fastened to the tail-piece of the Crupper.

To prevent the Bandage interfering with the staling of the Horse, an opening of a proper size may be made. This will be found very useful, as Compresses wetted with the Mixture can constantly be kept in contact with the Testicles.

When the Testicles hang very low,

without any Inflammation existing, dashing them with cold Water will be of use, and a Bandage applied for an hour once a day will tend to restore the strength of the power which naturally supports the Testicles.

OF THE CONTENTS OF THE CHEST.

No. I.

OINTMENT FOR WOUNDS.

This is to be spread rather thinly upon Tow, and applied as before directed to Wounds, Bruised Backs, when they have running Sores upon them, and to Ulcers in other parts of the body.

No. II.

POWDER FOR STRAINS, LAMENESS, &c.

Put two tea-spoonfulls of this into a bowl, stir it up with four table-spoonfulls of Malt Spirits or Brandy, add to it by degrees three half pints of soft Water, pour it into a bottle, and mix with it four table-spoonfulls of sharp Vinegar.

Wrung Withers, Bruised Backs, or Bowel Galls, ought to be frequently sponged with this Mixture, and covered (if the situation of the parts will admit of it) with folded cloths wetted with the same. Strained and Swelled Legs should be first well washed with it, and afterwards loosely bound up in folds of soft spongy old Linen, covered with a Bandage made of old stocking, thick flannel, or soft rug; the whole to be kept constantly moist, and renewed at least twice a day.

As much Powder as will lie on a

Half-rupee put to a pint of Rain or River Water, with a table-spoonfull of Brandy, will make a cooling Wash for Inflamed Eyes.

No. III.

DRYING POWDER.

This is to be used in every case of Sore where the flesh has risen to a level with the edges of the Skin, and should be sprinkled freely over it. When the Scab falls off, fresh Powder must be used, and so on till the Sore be healed.

If the new Flesh be higher than the edges of the Skin, mix the Powder with an equal quantity of burnt Alum ; when the surface is rendered level, use the Powder alone.

No. IV.

PURGING BALLS.

This size of Ball is calculated for a strong, full grown Horse.

If it purges too much, diminish one quarter; if not sufficiently, increase it as much.

Purges are of use in abating Inflammation, in cases of Worms, and where Horses fall off in condition, without any obvious cause.

They may be repeated for two or three times, according to the necessity of the case, leaving an interval of eight or nine days between two Doses.

The treatment of Horses before Physic consists in giving moist food, and that only in small quantities; and in keeping them rather warmer than usual during its Operation, allowing them much water, not quite cold.

No. V.

DIURETIC BALLS.

Each Ball is calculated, like the foregoing article, for a full grown strong Horse, &c.

They, as well as the Purgative Balls, are of very general use, and may, in slighter degrees of those cases in which the former are found serviceable, be substituted with advantage. In Swelled Legs, and Cracked Heels with slight Inflammation, they are found very beneficial, and also when given in half the usual quantity for Coughs of long standing.

No. VI.

CORDIAL, OR RESTORATIVE BALLS.

These fall under the same circumstances with the preceding; are particularly useful after hard riding, and when given fasting in a morning during long journies.

No. VII.

COLIC BALLS.

See the article Colic.

THRUSH MIXTURE.

See the article Running Thrushes.

DRYING MIXTURE.

See the article Treads and Over-reaches.

STYPTIC TINCTURE.

This is intended to stop the Flow of Blood from any part of a Wound. Sponge the Surface of the Wound, in order to discover the parts from which the Blood jets out.

Make a small Button of Tow, which dip in the Tincture, and apply to the bleeding Points; and over this place a second, somewhat larger, and press with the finger upon the part.

Should the Bleeding continue, warm a small quantity of the Tincture in a tea-cup, taking care to prevent its catching fire, and use it as before directed. If the first application fail to stop the Bleeding, repeat it two or three times.

When a very large vessel happens to be divided, and the use of the Tincture proves ineffectual, endeavour to tie the bleeding Ends with waxed Threads, which should hang out of the Wound; or the Ends of the Vessel may be touched with a hot Iron, if it do not run deep, or near Joints; in which case it would be well to call in the aid of a Surgeon.

TINCTURE FOR WOUNDS.

This is intended for fresh Flesh Wounds.

With a soft Sponge and warm Water cleanse the Surface of the Wound, but do not rub it hard. Having dipped some Tow in the Tincture, squeeze it half-dry and apply it to the Wound, so that it shall reach about an inch beyond the cut Edges, then cover the whole with dry Tow. This must be done whether the Wound be deep or shallow, without any Dressing being stuffed within. In case of profuse Bleeding, use the Styptic Tincture as before directed. A thin Flannel Roller should be loosely applied, if the Wound be in any part of the Leg; if in the upper part of the Body, where a Bandage cannot be used, let the Dressings be held on for half an hour by the hand, and afterwards cut narrow stripes of Sticking Plaster, of a sufficient length to reach an inch and a half beyond the Dressings ; warm them before the fire, and cross them in different directions, pressing the ends closely against the Skin.

Let them remain on as long as they will stick, unless either the discharge become very offensive, or in large quantity, or there be much soreness or swelling in the surrounding parts, or falling off from feeding, or Fever ; in which case use the Mixture made of the Powder (No. II.) as directed under that article.

Wash the parts well with it, apply Tow moistened, and over all folds of old soft Linen wetted with the same. As long as the soreness or swelling continues the Linen must be kept constantly wet, using no tighter bandage than may be necessary to keep on the Dressings. Should the swelling and soreness be great, from two to five quarts of Blood ought to be taken away, and a Purging Ball (No. IV.)

be given ; if they only exist in a slight degree a Diuretic Ball may prove sufficient. When the soreness and swelling go off, and the Sore discharges good matter, dress with the Digestive Ointment (No. I.) spread upon Tow once a day, or twice if the discharge be great.

When the new flesh springs from the bottom, and gets nearly to a level with the edges of the Wound, leave off the Ointment, and cover the surface with the Powder (No. III.) Let the scab fall off of itself. Repeat this as long as any Discharge continues.

OF THE DOSES OF THE MEDICINES.

The Masses are so composed, that an ounce of each forms a Dose for a full grown Horse.

In case they should grow hard, they may be beat up with Honey or Molasses.

OF THE THRUSH, AND DRYING MIXTURES.

The disposition to ferment is so strong in these Mixtures, as not to admit of their being sent into a hot climate in a complete state. The dry Ingredients are therefore alone put into the respective Bottles, and the following is the method of preparing them.

FOR THE THRUSH MIXTURE.

Put six ounces of Honey with three meat-spoonfulls of Vinegar into an earthen vessel, simmer them over a slow fire, and stir in the Powders, till the whole be thoroughly incorporated. When the liquid is nearly cold, cautiously add two drams of Nitrous Acid, which is easily procurable.

This should be kept in a large bottle; and that in the Chest should only be filled to one-third.

FOR THE DRYING MIXTURE.

Take three ounces of Honey and twelve meat-spoonfulls of Vinegar, simmer them together, and stir in the Powder.—This Mixture ferments less than the former; but the Chest Bottle should be not more than half filled.

N. B. Mr. Moorcroft would feel himself particularly obliged by any communication respecting the Diseases of Horses in India; and should the Chests he now sends be found deserving of encouragement, he purposes next year to form a more extensive Assortment, and to cause the Medicines contained in each to be deposited at Messrs. Lambert and Ross's, for the accommodation of such Gentlemen as may wish to replenish their Chests.